It's Christ...mas!
DAN COATES
Piano Favorites
For Advanced Piano

Ave Maria (Franz Shubert) **6**

The Birthday of a King **3**

Frosty the Snowman **10**

Gesù Bambino **22**

Grown Up Christmas List **14**

Have Yourself a Merry Little Christmas **19**

Here Comes Santa Claus (Right Down Santa Claus Lane) **26**

(There's No Place Like) Home for the Holidays **29**

It's the Most Wonderful Time of the Year **40**

Mary Did You Know? **32**

We Three Kings of Orient Are **36**

Project Manager: Carol Cuellar
Cover Design: Candy Woolley
Piano Photo: © 2002 Yamaha Corporation
DAN COATES® is a registered trademark of Warner Bros. Publications

Dan Coates ❑❑❑❑❑❑❑❑❑❑❑❑❑❑❑❑❑❑❑

As a student at the University of Miami, Dan Coates paid his tuition by playing the piano at south Florida nightclubs and restaurants. One evening in 1975, after Dan had worked his unique brand of magic on the ivories, a stranger from the music field walked up and told him that he should put his inspired piano arrangements down on paper so they could be published.

Dan took the stranger's advice—and the world of music has become much richer as a result. Since that chance encounter long ago, Dan has gone on to achieve international acclaim for his brilliant piano arrangements. His *Big Note, Easy Piano and Professional Touch* arrangements have inspired countless piano students and established themselves as classics against which all other works must be measured.

Enjoying an exclusive association with Warner Bros. Publications since 1982, Dan has demonstrated a unique gift for writing arrangements intended for students of every level, from beginner to advanced. Dan never fails to bring a fresh and original approach to his work. Pushing his own creative boundaries with each new manuscript, he writes material that is musically exciting and educationally sound.

From the very beginning of his musical life, Dan has always been eager to seek new challenges. As a five-year-old in Syracuse, New York, he used to sneak into the home of his neighbors to play their piano. Blessed with an amazing ear for music, Dan was able to imitate the melodies of songs he had heard on the radio. Finally, his neighbors convinced his parents to buy Dan his own piano. At that point, there was no stopping his musical development. Dan won a prestigious New York State competition for music composers at the age of 15. Then, after graduating from high school, he toured the world as an arranger and pianist with the group Up With People.

Later, Dan studied piano at the University of Miami with the legendary Ivan Davis, developing his natural abilities to stylize music on the keyboard. Continuing to perform professionally during and after his college years, Dan has played the piano on national television and at the 1984 Summer Olympics in Los Angeles. He has also accompanied recording artists as diverse as Dusty Springfield and Charlotte Rae.

During his long and prolific association with Warner Bros. Publications, Dan has written many awardwinning books. He conducts piano workshops worldwide, demonstrating his famous arrangements with a special spark that never fails to inspire students and teachers alike.

THE BIRTHDAY OF A KING

By
WILLIAM HAROLD NEIDLINGER
Arranged by DAN COATES

Moderately, with expression (♩ = 100)

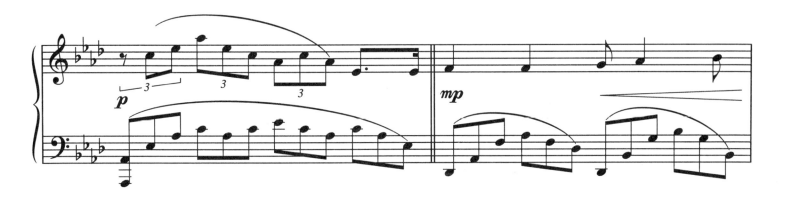

THE BIRTHDAY OF A KING

By
WILLIAM HAROLD NEIDLINGER
Arranged by DAN COATES

Moderately, with expression (♩ = 100)

The Birthday of a King - 3 - 1

AVE MARIA

FRANZ SCHUBERT, Op. 52
Arranged by DAN COATES

Slowly, with reverence

Ave Maria- 4 - 1

FROSTY THE SNOWMAN

Words and Music by
STEVE NELSON and
JACK ROLLINS
Arranged by DAN COATES

Brightly (♩ = 80)

Frosty the Snowman - 4 - 1

cresc. poco a poco

GROWN-UP CHRISTMAS LIST

Words and Music by
DAVID FOSTER and
LINDA THOMPSON JENNER
Arranged by DAN COATES

Grown-up Christmas List - 5 - 1

16

18

HAVE YOURSELF
A MERRY LITTLE CHRISTMAS

Words and Music by
HUGH MARTIN and RALPH BLANE
Arranged by DAN COATES

Slowly, with expression

Have Yourself a Merry Little Christmas - 3 - 1

Have Yourself a Merry Little Christmas - 3 - 3

GESÙ BAMBINO
(The Infant Jesus)

Words by
FREDERICK H. MARTENS
Italian Version by
PIETRO A. YON

Music by
PIETRO A. YON
Arranged by DAN COATES

Moderately slow (♩. = 66)

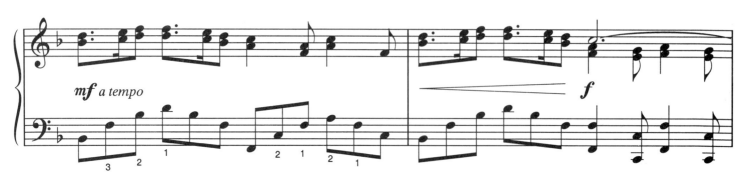

Gesù Bambino - 4 - 1

(not too slowly)

ff   *p*   *espressivo*

cresc.   *mp*

mf

Gesù Bambino- 4 - 4

HERE COMES SANTA CLAUS
(Right Down Santa Claus Lane)

Words and Music by
GENE AUTRY and OAKLEY HALDEMAN
Arranged by DAN COATES

Here Comes Santa Claus - 3 - 1

(There's No Place Like)
HOME FOR THE HOLIDAYS

Words by
AL STILLMAN

Music by
ROBERT ALLEN
Arranged by DAN COATES

Home for the Holidays - 3 - 1

D.S. %al Coda

✆ *Coda*

MARY, DID YOU KNOW?

Words and Music by
MARK LOWRY and BUDDY GREENE
Arranged by DAN COATES

Reverently (♩ = 100)

(with pedal)

(L.H. simile)

Mary, Did You Know? - 4 - 1

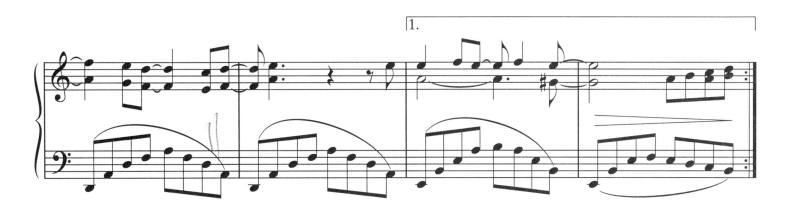

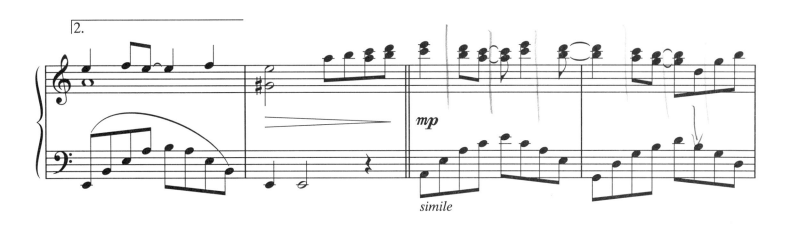

Mary, Did You Know? - 4 - 2

Mary, Did You Know? - 4 - 3

WE THREE KINGS OF ORIENT ARE

Words and Music by
JOHN HENRY HOPKINS
Arranged by DAN COATES

Not too slow

We Three Kings of Orient Are - 4 - 1

38

We Three Kings of Orient Are - 4 - 3

IT'S THE MOST WONDERFUL TIME OF THE YEAR

By EDDIE POLA and
GEORGE WYLE
Arranged by DAN COATES

Bright jazz waltz

It's the Most Wonderful Time of the Year - 5 - 1

42

It's the Most Wonderful Time of the Year - 5 - 3

44

It's the Most Wonderful Time of the Year - 5 - 5